DISCOVER YOUR WRITER'S VOICE
WORKBOOK

By
Alice  Crider
your write life coach

Discover Your Writer's Voice Workbook by Alice Crider
www.alicecrider.com

Cover Designer: Melissa Macis
Editor: Kimberly Shumate
Typesetter: Jeff Gerke, www.jeffgerke.com

International Standard Book Number (13): 9781072491743

Printed in the United States of America

CONTENTS

1	Introduction
5	What Is a Writer's Voice?
	• Exercise 1: Brain Dump on Paper
	• Exercise 2: Identify Their Mood
	• Exercise 3: Describe Your Mood
21	Get in the Zone!
23	Motives and an Audience of One
	• Exercise 4: Complete Your Book's Target Audience Template
27	No Judgment
31	Writing Compelling Dialogue
	• Exercise 5: Coffee that Cures Bad Dialogue
35	Do I Have More Than One Voice?
	• Exercise 6: Hear It Out Loud
41	Writing Is Art, Publishing Is a Business
43	Think Tribe, Not Platform
	• Exercise 7: Pushing the Boundaries
47	Conclusion: Write On!
49	Appendix A

INTRODUCTION

Your writing voice is the deepest possible reflection of who you are. The job of your voice is not to seduce or flatter or make well-shaped sentences. In your voice, your readers should be able to hear the contents of your mind, your heart, your soul.

—MEG ROSOFF

I've been meaning to sit down and write this book for a ridiculously long time. Apparently, I needed to learn how to spell *procrastination* first. Can you relate? I've always had a fascination with words, and I used to dream of being a real writer, an author of books people would cherish.

But when I attended my first writers' conference a few decades ago, I had a rather discouraging epiphany: book writing is a business! I wasn't so sure I wanted to start a business. I just wanted to play with words. I also heard authors and editors talk about the importance of "voice" . . . and they said you had to write for a long time—as in *years*—in order to find your voice. It all sounded so difficult!

Later at the same conference, as I sat listening to a panel of editors talk about how great their jobs were, I became fascinated. Being an editor looked like a journey that if committed to, I could learn, grow, and become a part of a creative team making a difference in the world at the same time making a living for myself. I decided right then to become an editor.

As I began the process, I quickly realized that it *looked* much easier than it actually was. I definitely had to learn a lot of things the hard way, and once I was almost fired for a job I wasn't entirely qualified for. Now, years later, I can tell you that at times, publishing is hard for everybody, no matter who you are. Nobody ever totally "arrives" until you get to heaven and find out how well you really did. The journey, whether you ever publish a book or not, will challenge and stretch you. And it's all worth the cost if you don't quit.

As an acquisitions editor for a traditional publishing house, my job is to find authors with three foundational elements: a unique concept, a platform, and excellent writing.

As a writer, whether you self-publish or go with a traditional publisher, and whether you're writing fiction or nonfiction, you need those same things to give you a competitive advantage in today's market.

My intention is that this workbook will enable you to become the very best writer you personally can be. Because, guess what? Your voice isn't lost so it doesn't need to be found. Your voice is within you, waiting to be discovered, and it doesn't have to take years!

Within these pages, you'll have the opportunity to:

- Discover how to couple your artistic inner aspirations with fundamental writing tools that will help you produce unique and compelling pages
- Tap into your personal inner genius
- Develop your own exclusive style that reflects what only you can say
- Reel in your readers with a tone and tempo they can identify with while still enjoying a new and vibrant narrative

This guidebook offers substantial exercises to promote the skills you'll need as a writer in order to compete in today's literary market. (We can discuss platform elsewhere.) Now, grab your favorite beverage, get comfortable, and breathe in the discovery that is your writer's voice!

How to Use This Workbook

At the very beginning of every book ever written was a parcel of time solely dedicated to the purpose of conceptualizing—hammering out—the author's manuscript idea. And so it is for you and this workbook. It's the essential stage where imagination meets realization and what's known as the creative process. Left brain versus right brain and sometimes the war between the two. If you've ever wondered why the creative you (living in your right hemisphere) struggles with the intellectual you (living next door in the left), it's easy to explain. Writing—good writing—takes both of you. But for fun, let's see what happens when we separate your left from right.

The right side of our brain inspires our art awareness, creativity, imagination, intuition, insight, holistic thought, music appreciation, and so on. It's the mother of all tasty treats wafting from the kitchen. It's the kid coloring so far outside the lines, it's not clear anymore what the original picture was supposed to be. It's the over-the-top home decorator who insists that gold lamé drapes do *not* clash with chartreuse throw pillows. You get the picture. The right hemisphere of the brain fills our heart and soul with all that is colorful, magical, and wondrous. It feeds our fancies and brings life to our dreams.

How about the left side of our brain and the part it plays in our daily lives? It controls our analytical thought, logic, language, memory, reasoning, decision making, science, math, and yes, writing! It stores our roadmaps and internal voicemail. But most importantly to us as wordsmiths, it rules our hand-eye coordination. For any job requiring our hands, such as drawing, typing, or handwriting (to name only a few), the brain's left side is needed.

That means in order to reconcile our two warring sides, they must come to terms with one another—an agreement that they will take turns in the creative process. This workbook is for both sides of you. And what better way to begin your stellar literary work than to come to that arrangement before the fireworks start to fly. The best way I know how—tested by many established authors of past and present—is to write by hand.

In the coming exercises, I invite you to leave the computer behind to embrace the almighty pen (or pencil). Why? Because handwriting takes your mind to a more relaxed state. It allows for delay—precious time for your right side to stroll, to gaze up, to reflect back, to collect mental images, and to take writing at a leisurely pace. Don't worry if your writing style looks sloppy, lacks finesse, loses grammar, or slides off course. That's the point. Give yourself permission to be imperfect.

Think of it this way: A document begins in a perfect state. It's white, shiny with crisp lines and margins. It catches spelling errors and is constantly tapping its fingernail in the form of an ever-blinking curser for you to hurry up and move on. After a while, you realize your writing isn't quite living up to the bar set for it by your techno partner. But with swoops, swirls, sketches, or simply your own familiar chicken scratches eked out on the page, suddenly you're in very comfortable territory with your mind free and your creative juices flowing.

In the exercises ahead, first use the writing space provided in this workbook. If you run out of room, grab a journal, a notepad, or scratch paper and keep going. I promise there is something to be discovered in this method.

WHAT IS A WRITER'S VOICE?

If you were to ask a number of bestselling authors how they discovered their writing voice, most of them would probably tell you they don't really know. They just write how they think. But that's not all there is to it.

At the risk of sounding romantic, your writer's voice is your heart and soul on paper. It's you being authentic and transparent about what you think, believe, feel, and know. Sure, you may be writing nonfiction that's loaded with research, stats, and formulas that explain a position or back up a message, but you can still have a voice in it. Some experts say it takes years to hone your voice, but I don't believe that.

Academic and curricular writing versus creative writing (be it fiction or nonfiction) is the perfect example of how these two worlds collide. Someone writing their dissertation can sound cold, antiseptic, and inaccessible. You'll notice very little feeling, but lots of facts and forecasts. You have no idea what the writer is like personally—their disposition as a human being—and that's a problem if a writer is attempting to engage the reader with a distinct energy on the page. One that is easily recognizable. It's called *voice*.

Because they are familiar with scholastic writing, some authors feel the need to keep things sharp, colorless, and perfect. But writing is not a perfect art form. Some literary works aren't written all that well, but they have immense appeal due to the voice on the page and the emotional connection with the audience. A great example is *The Notebook*. Not a literary masterpiece, but a gigantic success for Nicholas Sparks. If you browse your local library, I'm sure you'll find plenty more.

The Fine Line Between Author and Voice

Let's talk about the difference between your reader hearing you the writer—one who carefully crafts each word, sentence, paragraph, chapter—and your reader hearing the real you on the page. Aren't they the same thing? Definitely not. As an editor, I have a pet peeve of an author trying too hard to impress. Suddenly, I've lost track of the character(s), the story, and/or the meaning of the book within the self-serving validation of the author begging to be noticed. I can almost hear her. "Look at this sentence! Check out these words placed so carefully together to make one perfect thought. But wait, I'm about to do it again. Aren't I amazing?"

Okay, that was a little much, but I bet you're nodding your head. We all want to be an incredible wordsmith who rises above the masses. However, trying to be perfect isn't going to do anything for you but silence your true voice and paralyze your gift of being you. I hate to drop the bomb, but you are not perfect. And how interesting or relatable would you be to others if you were?

My suggestion: Be yourself. Don't aim for perfection; commit to authenticity instead.

How Will You Know When You've Found Your Voice?

First of all, don't Google it. It isn't an app that you can simply look up, download, plug in, and wham! You've got *voice*!

You'll know you've tapped into your writer's voice when you're suddenly surprised by something you just wrote. You'll feel tickled, amused, and maybe a little curious about where the words and sentences just came from. You might get a warm, comforting sensation deep inside, a kind of "knowing" that something is very *right*. You might feel excited and catch yourself being slightly intimidated. You might wonder, *Did I really just write that?*

Revel in that moment. Cling to it. Keep writing as long as you can; as long as your fingers find the keys and your eyes can stand the glare of the page or screen—as long as the jubilation lasts. Ride it out . . . you've just found your voice!

Only *you* can bring out your own writer's voice. Nobody else can do *you* as you can. But getting back to what voice is, I think the easiest thing to do is first talk about what voice isn't.

VOICE *IS NOT* . . .

- Flowery or fluffy writing
- Something you can force
- A style of writing, though sometimes it may seem that way
- Being smart, exceptionally articulate, clever, or controlled
- You talking

Granted, some readers like fluff, and there are definitely certain genres that lend themselves to it more than others—gift books, whimsical romances, poetry, literary classics. But fluff isn't voice; it's a style of writing. It's not an identity or sound. It's like pink floral wallpaper. It may be pretty to look at, but it doesn't say a lot.

If you try to force your voice, most of the time it comes off as shouting—figuratively speaking. And no one enjoys being shouted at. We prefer a much kinder, welcoming tone to bring us into a conversation. Not to say that your voice can't, at times, be strong, persuasive, or dynamic. It simply means that settling into your true voice on the page will allow it to unfold organically as the genuine article that will resonate with readers.

Style is another animal entirely. Spots. Stripes. Scales. All different. However, those are not voice. Anyone can learn a style and many people do. Then what happens? They all end up sounding like each other. That's why we love reading Jane Austen, listening to Elton John, or watching *The Wizard of Oz*. Yes, they all have a recognizable style, but deeper still, they have their own soul. No one else writes like Shakespeare. No one else sings like Barbara Streisand. No other movie offers a POV (point of view) like *Titanic*. They're all great, and they all have their own flavor, not formula.

Voice is not style, it's substance.

In the same vein, it's not how much you know, but how you say what you do know. With enough research and study, anyone can sound educated, fluent, or even profound. But how many high school or university classes did you fall asleep in while listening to teachers and professors drone on in lecture halls? I could even argue that if not delivered thoughtfully and with a fresh and relevant take, curriculum and scholastic works can be the nighttime sedative you've been looking for. Five minutes of audio, and you're rendered totally unconscious. You might be listening to a voice, but it's not the kind of *voice* you want.

Finally, if *talking* were voice, then I would have no need to write this book. Publishers would have the easiest job in the world. And literary agents would be out of a job completely. No, the voice on the page is not talking as we do in everyday life. Voice is more like you, thinking. Most people talk without thinking, but page voice is your having original thoughts the way you *think* them, not necessarily the way you'd say them out loud.

Now let's look at what voice actually is.

VOICE IS . . .

- Your personality on paper
- Your presence in the mind of your audience as they read
- Your words offered as a meaningful connection—to help, humor, encourage, teach, etc.
- Your speaking directly and personally to your reader—because you care

Have you ever read a book or even a letter written by someone you know well? Did you notice how you actually hear their voice? Such as when a close friend calls you on the phone and in one word you know exactly who it is. Weird, right? It's their tone, their pitch. And it's the inflection of personality that is unique only to them, like a fingerprint or birthmark.

That's what you're going to discover about your own voice in this workbook. Your true note as only you can sing it. A personal discussion you initiate in writing that leaves a lasting mark.

So, what is voice? It is your passion, your spirit and soul, your presence in the words—words that reach your reader's heart because you are opening and sharing yours.

Where does voice come from besides your heart? I've worked with a number of different authors who insist that their writing sounds like how they talk and that's how their voice is. But now we know that's not necessarily true. Sure, every author has a basic vocabulary and vernacular they write from, and some have cultural phrases that are relevant to what they write. But the origin of voice comes from vulnerability and authenticity, not the dictionary. It comes from being open and gut-level honest. Sharing the dark side as well as the light. It's a relationship between you and your audience. Spending time with them—one imperfect human with another. Stepping into their world and inviting them into yours.

Transparency . . . it's a beautiful thing. What you think, what you believe, what you experience, convey completely yet invisibly . . . through your voice.

WHY IS IT IMPORTANT TO HAVE A VOICE ON THE PAGE?

If voice is your presence on paper, then it's only fair to the reader that he hear you—know whom they're sharing company with, who is communicating with them, who is taking them on a journey. It allows them to embrace you with their time and trust—which is precious and should never be taken for granted. You write to educate and to entertain. You want people to remember what you wrote, so you need to say it distinctively enough that your words, concepts, and stories stick with them. Perhaps for life.

As I mentioned before, many writers are so focused on their message or on writing complex sentences that it takes a long time to settle into their unique voice. This first exercise will help you discover your own unusual expression. It will help you stand out as an author, and also ripple out as you build your tribe of readers.

EXERCISE 1: *BRAIN DUMP ON PAPER*

 I learned this writing exercise when I took a stand-up comedy workshop a few years ago. I took the class because I wanted to become a better speaker. In the process, I learned more about writing than I ever have in my 20+ years of book editing.

Here's how it works. Take a few minutes and allow your mind to wonder. Think about your day, last week, a friend (or someone who's not so friendly), the bug on your shoe, the tickle in your throat. If it helps, put on some music that inspires your creative juices and just wander.

For the next five minutes, make a list of everything you thought about. I promise, you think about more than you're conscious of. Nothing is off limits. In fact, if you censor yourself, you'll miss out on the benefits of this exercise. Everything from the weather to food to intimate relationships, politics, career, health, and what kind of dog food you're thinking of buying at the store. List hairstyles or baldness, fitness or chronic illness, etc.

List absolutely everything you think about. You can use single words or phrases or even questions. You can list memories or thoughts about the future. Keep it simple but specific enough that you can look back later and know what you meant.

Write until something comes out of you that totally surprises you. Dig deep into your thoughts and emotions as you write. You might get angry, feel sad, laugh, or think you're going nowhere, but keep writing.

Don't write a paragraph, and do not start working on your current literary piece, book, chapter, or blog. Simply bullet-point the snapshots that come to mind. When you've run out of thoughts, pause for a few seconds then keep writing. Seriously, don't stop! By this point, your brain is just getting started. Write down anything more that comes to you.

Ready? Set a timer for five minutes and write here:

_____

_____

_____

_____

_____

_____

_____

_____

_____

_____

_____

_____

_____

_____

_____

_____

_____

_____

Next, look at your list and circle three things that have some kind of emotional charge. Something that makes you say, *Oh, my gosh, that makes me so mad,* or *Wow, I'm in love with my husband,* or *My children drive me crazy,* or something that totally scares you. Look for the standouts, the most riveting.

Once you've chosen your three favorites, pick one that you're willing to write about. Not something that has anything to do with a current writing project. You'll tend to want to control it. You need to be out of control for this exercise to work!

Finished?

Now, for the next ten minutes, write on your chosen topic—everything that comes to mind around that one thing. You're going to do some freewheeling that gets you going emotionally. If you happen to be writing a memoir and there's some traumatic memory of your past that you want to write about, just cover the specific memory and nothing else.

As you write, consider some of the following questions meant to trigger thoughts about your topic:

What's the best thing about my topic?

What's the worst thing about it?

What's the scariest thing or the most incredible thing?

What's working and what's not?

What does the future look like because of this thing?

What do I think it means?

Get to where you've run out of things to say, then go back and push yourself a little further. Challenge yourself by digging in deeper. You might even talk to God about it and say, "Okay God, what else is here?" and let Him guide you into a richer place where you're super vulnerable.

No one is going to read this unless you want to share it. Right now, you're writing for an audience of one—we'll touch on that a little further on. But at this moment, it's just you (and God if you invite Him into this session). It's time to get real. Go where you might be afraid to go; step into uncertainty. That's where you'll find the good stuff. It's this kind of writing that when continually practiced, brings out who you truly are. Which is what? Your *voice*.

Ready? Set a timer for ten minutes and write here now:

_____

_____

_____

_____

_____

_____

_____

_____

_____

_____

_____

_____

_____

_____

_____

_____

_____

_____

_____

_____

_____

_____

_____

_____

_____

_____

_____

_____

_____

_____

_____

_____

_____

_____

_____

_____

_____

_____

_____

_____

_____

_____

Now stop and look at what you've written. Kind of wild, huh? Hopefully, you found yourself in a part of your life you haven't seen before, or maybe just from a different angle. Perhaps a completely fresh and innovative thought occurred. An "aha" moment. An epiphany. A premise that came out of *your* mind—the only mind that could have thought it.

By the end of this *brain dump*, you'll have discovered a brand-new gear and tapped that all-important right brain. And the longer you stay there—amidst the whirl of artistic expression—you will begin to find home. The residence where your writer lives.

The birthplace of voice.

Note: If you did not have that experience, you can either keep writing until you do, or set this workbook aside and do the exercise again at a later time.

Consider Your State of Mind

When reading literature, if you really pay attention, you can tell what kind of mood a writer was in when she sat down to write it. Nostalgic, excited, sad, silly, cerebral, spiritual, introverted or extroverted.

Exercise 2: *Identify Their Mood*

Look at some examples that reveal the mood of the following authors within the first line(s) of chapter one. Pick a word that best describes the emotional state of that author, then write it on the line below. And don't worry: there are no right or wrong answers.

- It was a wrong number that started it, the telephone ringing three times in the dead of night, and the voice on the other end asking for someone he was not. —Paul Auster, *City of Glass* (1985)

_____

_____

_____

- Once upon a time, there was a woman who discovered she had turned into the wrong person. —Anne Tyler, *Back When We Were Grownups* (2001)

_____

_____

- And so it had come to this. Horrified as he stood on a height above the Potomac, James Madison, the fourth President of the United States—and now, some wondered, the last?—watched his beloved Washington City as it seemed to vanish into a crimson-orange swirl of fire. —Michael Beschloss, *Presidents War* (2018)

_____

_____

- You better not never tell nobody but God. —Alice Walker, *The Color Purple* (1982)

_____

_____

- Granted: I am an inmate of a mental hospital; my keeper is watching me, he never lets me out of his sight . . . —Gunter Grass, *The Tin Drum* (1959)

_____

_____

- I write this sitting in the kitchen sink. —Dodie Smith, *I Capture the Castle* (1948)

_____

_____

- I worked mornings at the cemetery and nights at the gas station, and if I could have found a third [expletive] job, I would have taken it in my futile quest to stay busy and not think about the fact that my girlfriend was living on a commune in Vermont (or was it New Hampshire?) with a bunch of hippies while I was living at home with my disappointed parents and my little brother and sisters. —David Noonan, *Attempted Hippie* (2014)

_____

_____

I'm sure you had no problem assigning an adjective to each sentence. See how quickly the mood was set and the author's voice was heard? So much personality. Thick with intrigue. Nothing vanilla about them. That's what a great voice can bring to your work.

EXERCISE 3: *DESCRIBE YOUR MOOD*

Now think about how you're feeling when you sit down to write. What does your internal vibe feel like? Does it vary or pretty much stay in the same key? One tone, several, or none?

Read a few pages of something you've written, and list the words that best describe the feeling or emotions that represent your mood within the work.

_____

_____

_____

Examples: Passionate, depressed, naïve, hopeful, hysterical, joyful, paranoid, vulnerable, etc.

Now, which voice or adjective describes you the best?

_____

_____

Which one brings your personality with it?

_____

_____

Got it? Now hold true to it. Keep it close to you like a friend who has your back. Let that voice resound in the way you share your ideas on the page. Let it echo like a clap of thunder. Let it shake the foundation of the one who reads it. Let it be entirely and unmistakably *you*.

GET IN THE ZONE!

What do you need in order to find your groove? A cozy room, soft music, velvet lighting . . . dreamy. If it takes your favorite writer's chair, moth-eaten wool sweater, or that perfect cup of herbal tea or glass of Chardonnay to get you in the mood, so be it. Find that happy place and fall into it. Redirect all of your senses so accustomed to the hurly-burly race outside and slow them down; quiet them; take possession of them. Then, set them free.

Your zone should not include those authors that came before you or happen to currently occupy your bookcase or the shelves of Barnes Noble. Not to say that snuggling into one of those inviting, over-stuffed chairs surrounded by the smell of hardbacks, trade paper, and sensational cover art can't inspire and ignite me to write. It does, and I often find myself there.

Just beware that with those armies of books (listening, watching, judging), you might be tempted to try to impersonate your favorite (famous) voices rich with their own tenor. But that's not what "getting in the zone" is about. It means pushing out all that distracts you from your involuntary or subliminal expression within. That's the matter that can only be found in your personal mental landscape. No freeloaders allowed. It's just you and your voice. That's it.

For me, it's all about losing myself in the void. Not the emptiness or vacuum we usually associate with that word, but the place where everything "normal" is pushed out and filled with a multicolored mixture of my own making. Whatever comes to me as my mind wonders, listening to my favorite instrumental music streaming through my headphones. (I can't listen to songs with lyrics lest I stop writing and start singing.) Or the words and phrases that flow from my second cup of bulletproof coffee.

Try new things. Discover what speaks to you. Music that reflects the story's subject or theme; a fragrance or taste that transports you; the texture of an artsy gifted journal that always releases your inner-visionary. Whatever it is, lay claim and live there.

And just when you're not paying too much attention, the writing will begin to flow and you'll hear your voice coming through. When you find yourself elated by your own thoughts pouring out through your keyboard or pen, you're in the zone. It might even feel like you're channeling some genius, but that's actually you. You are the prodigy. You just had to find your way home. Give yourself permission to dismiss the world—if only for a couple of hours—and enjoy the mental real estate that is . . . the zone.

Not enough time? I get that. For years I thought I didn't have time to write, and one day I decided to give myself fifteen minutes to see how far I could get. I set my kitchen timer, put on my headphones, and let the Piano Guys transport me out of my immediate surroundings. An hour later I'd written several pages and my busy life hadn't imploded without me. Since then, I've snatched many fifteen-minute segments of writing bliss, some of which went longer, most of which were cut short. And that's how this book landed in your hands.

Try it yourself, and create your own zone!

MOTIVES AND AN AUDIENCE OF ONE

When you think about your audience, consider this: before pondering the mass market or a smaller indie following, write to one person. Ideally to yourself. I say this to diminish your inner censor—your built-in editor who loves to dictate your content. Of course, it's absolutely necessary to write appropriately to the readers who will purchase your book. But right now, let's just concentrate on you.

What makes you happy? What life lesson are you needing to therapeutically put down on paper—for yourself? What demons are you exercising, love are you relishing, loss you are grieving? Is your memoir driven by an arc of pain and redemption? Does your fictional story weave a thread of hope and healing? Does your nonfiction or self-help work offer tangible examples and takeaway value?

If you can't answer yes to these questions, then you should rethink your motives for writing. Because if you don't need these questions answered for you, then your material has no place to rest—not in you or in anyone else. But if you can find the "yes" in your personal reasons for writing, then writing for yourself first and foremost will keep your material pure and untainted by market value. Creating an original, authentic piece of work will carry its own weight out in the world.

After you've come to terms with your motives for writing, then it's time to think about your reader—your target audience. Much like having a conversation face-to-face, it's important to ask your reader questions or at the very least, instill the curiosity in them to find questions and answers of their own. Suddenly, your book becomes much more than just words, and reading it creates meaningful change.

WHO ARE YOU WRITING TO?

Audience. It's so important to know your audience, arguably the second most significant thing after nailing your voice. With your voice being a combination of how you think and how your audience listens, you must know your audience before you can speak to them. If you don't know them, your writing may come off as your talking *at* them instead of *to* them. Your writing voice gives your reader the illusion that you're sitting next to them, having a personal conversation with them.

Figuring out who your target audience is really isn't as complicated as some make it. Within every industry standard book proposal is a section titled Target Audience. This usually is comprised of two sub-headers: Primary Audience and Secondary Audience. Here's an example.

Book Title: *In Stitches: A Quilter's Guide to a Lifetime of Laughter*
Target Audience:

Primary . . .

- Women ages 22 to 55
- Professional quilters and seamstresses
- Home crafters and fabric aficionados who enjoy clean jokes

Secondary . . .

- Those needing stress relief through colorful, creative humor
- People looking for the perfect gift for a quilter or seamstress
- DIYers needing a good belly-laugh

Once you get started, it's easy to systematically think through the process by demographics (physical and locational characteristics) and by psychographics (attitudes, beliefs, and mental states). Consider each group and how they move and interact within their sphere of influence. What are their interests, activities, and opinions? What do they like or don't like? How do they think or reason? What do they believe (or disbelieve) and how does that connect with your topic or story? And what are they looking for within the pages of your book? Every reader has a "felt-need" and an actual need. It's your job to realize both and address them deftly, accurately, and thoughtfully.

You can even go a step further and consider things that will help you choose references that fit well within the composition: movies, food, literature, social expressions, music, hobbies, clubs or groups, attitude, philosophy, priorities, fears or phobias, sentimental soft spots, challenges, and goals.

Answering these questions will provide such valuable information about your audience that the connection between the two of you will happen quickly and conclusively. Remember, you're speaking directly to them, but *them* is really one—a single reader investing his time into your work. It's your responsibility to get to know them first, pouring a durable foundation that you can build upon in the months and years of books written especially for them.

As you research and resolve to truly know your reader, the end result gives you your audience. In the case of the example given, I would be writing to a target audience that embraces quilting, enjoys handcrafted arts, and sews, as well as people looking for comic relief within their hobby niche. But more than this, I understand their emotional connection to what they do: why they do it and what they get from it. Is it a family tradition? Is it well-crafted therapy? Is it simply because it brings them joy? It could be all three and many more. And because I've thought it through, I now have a clear picture of who will be reading my book and how I can reach them with my own personal bent—humor, creativity, and takeaway value.

EXERCISE 4: *COMPLETE YOUR BOOK'S TARGET AUDIENCE TEMPLATE*

Book Title:

Target Audience:

Primary . . .

-
-
-

Secondary . . .

-
-
-

That's awesome! And if you're writing for yourself, then you already know your audience, because it's you! That's why writing for you is the foremost important thing. The added benefit is that you already have an in-depth knowledge of your readers and know how to reach them emotionally. This is where the old adage "write what you know" makes complete sense.

If by chance you're writing about a topic that requires research or a measure of practiced empathy, then immerse yourself in that topic until it feels like second nature. Live there until you become part of it, or at least understand it to your full potential. It will only serve to bring you closer to your audience and your voice on the page.

NO JUDGMENT

No one likes to be judged, unless they're in a competition and running in first place. But we're talking about writing, and nothing kills a unique and truly special voice more quickly than judgment—that of your own or from someone else. It's a bad idea to judge your voice or your style. Writers have a tendency to love details, but we forget we're only human and that we are as broken as the next person. We strive for perfection only to come up short again and again. What's up with that?

Do yourself a favor: lighten up! Play. Leave self-consciousness in a box outside your writing space. Write fast without judging your words, grammar, punctuation, or anything else that requires the left side of your brain. Don't be cruel to your creative mind as it's running about, frolicking in the daisies. Don't bottle it up or hold it under the relentless weight of skepticism. Be your own champion. Have faith in your writing if only to explore new fields of expression, exotic buds of conversation, and unfamiliar paths that could well lead to your very best voice on paper.

Accept the fact that you are unique, competent at being you, and exceptionally great at it. No judgment. No doubts. Just willing to try something new. Write something different. Be the untamed version of all you can be. That's your voice!

Don't Shoot Yourself in the Foot–Clichés Are a Killer

Now we're on to one of my all-time worst pet peeves—clichés. There is nothing that will scream "I'm green!!!" to an editor or agent louder than the use of clichés. But instead of addressing the painfully long list here, take a look at a comprehensive directory of more than 500 clichés found at www.be-a-better-writer.com/cliches.html. This group of audacious offenders habitually hired by lay writers will prove just how easy it is to commit a felony without realizing it. Note that even within this impressive lineup, I noticed some still missing, like "It's not over till the fat lady sings." Not sure how that one got by them, but beware. If you've "heard [something] a hundred times" then it doesn't belong in your manuscript.

Essence Over Eloquence

Have you ever thought that voice might be the sheer volume of what you say on the page? As if you wrote enough content, the writing would somehow just emulate who you are as a writer. I think some authors write way too much because they hope that by page 500, the reader will *get them*.

In my editorial opinion and in the world of traditional publishing, *less* rather than more is always appreciated. When I receive a book proposal in which the author's manuscript has a word count of 100,000, the first thing I think is *overkill*. Then, if the writing is truly good, I think the document (unbeknownst to the author) probably contains Book #1 of a series plus 20,000 words of Book #2 included. But that's rarely the case. It's usually the writer being excessive. And if you saw the in-box of editors and agents, you would understand how quickly that sort of wordiness can be ignored.

Remember, less is more. Natural, not contrived. Editors, agents, and readers can smell manufactured or predictable writing because it *schtinks*. And no amount of flowery writing will make it smell any better. Instead, keep your writing concise.

A great exercise to practice concise, well-organized writing is to try condensing your story or topic into a magazine-style article consisting of no more than 700 to 1,000 words. Yes, that's all you get! Read articles and blogs for good examples—ones that capture your attention quickly, hold tightly to your interest, and conclude with your questions answered and your appetite satisfied. Use words that enhance what you're writing about rather than detract from it. Take advantage of active verbs that are more powerful vs. passive verbs that weaken the impact. (See Appendix A for examples of active and passive verbs.)

Consider taking a screenwriting class if you really want to learn the art of word economy. You'll get 100 sparse pages to tell a complete story, one in which every line and every word either provide important information about the character(s) or propel the plot forward. If it doesn't do one of those two things, it's unforgiveable because it's a waste of valuable space.

Look at your manuscript—at every page, paragraph, sentence, and words within those sentences. Are they all absolutely necessary to tell your story? Are you including small details and using your reader's limited memory to express something that would best be told with a single line of dialogue? Be kind to the reader by thoughtfully composing your literary portrait to include only what is needed and wanted by those taking the time to gaze through your lens.

WRITING COMPELLING DIALOGUE

And since we're on the subject of less is more, what better place to discuss dialogue when considering your voice on the page. This isn't just how your writer's voice sounds, but how your characters sound through speech and/or inner thoughts. I've come to the conclusion after decades of reading books containing dialogue that there is a natural cadence to speaking on paper. It either sounds natural (probably because the writer is a good listener) or really awkward (because the writer hasn't mastered the art of picking up on the nuances of speech).

When someone is present and really listening, the words settle into their psyche and become a part of them. Others think about yesterday or tomorrow and miss what's being said today. The best way to gain an understanding of dialogue is to live consciously.

Now, get ready for your voice to change when writing dialogue, especially since it must speak for more than one person. It's a good idea to create character bios with their emotional state and personal ticks. Are they educated? Are they shy or outgoing? Do they chatter in a hurry or talk so slowly people get irritated with them? It's really funny how small things like these affect how a person communicates. Keep track and be aware of your characters' traits as you give them a voice.

EXERCISE 5: *COFFEE THAT CURES BAD DIALOGUE*

Okay, it doesn't have to be coffee or even tea. It could be pizza. Just go find a place to sit for a while and just listen. Listen to all of the different people around you and how they act and react to each other. Notice how they ask questions and how simple or complicated their answers are. There are all kinds of characters out there, and some are downright hilarious. Just listen.

Take your laptop or a pen and paper, and jot down a conversation. Don't feel guilty. This isn't audible voyeurism. If they're out in public speaking loudly enough for you to hear them, chances are the conversation is not all that confidential. Unless, of course, you hear them whisper the words, "bank heist."

Once you have a full conversation written down, go through it and delete what doesn't offer insight into the person or move the essence of the subject forward. As a rule, human beings talk way more than needed in order to convey an idea, suggestion, information, or argument. When writing dialogue, be aware of how few words are needed to get your point across, then tighten the screws by leaving much of it out, some of which can even be facts. The last thing you want to do is spoon-feed your readers. Intrigue them; don't saturate them. You can answer nagging questions later in the story, if only to keep the reader turning the pages.

At the end of this dictation session should be a short—I stress the word *short*—conversation on the page that excludes fluff like these:

"Hi, how are you?"

"Oh, I'm fine. What would you like to drink? I hear the double mochachino is excellent here."

"I'm sorry," he said to the woman with the baby stroller, "but this seat is taken."

Your written dialogue should only include what is relevant to the story, what paints an accurate picture of what you want your reader to see in your character, and the exchange of conversation that sounds exactly how people really talk.

Good dialogue is one literary beverage that may take time acquiring a taste for but is definitely one worth a seat at Starbucks.

_____

_____

_____

_____

_____

_____

_____

_____

_____

_____

_____

_____

_____

DO I HAVE MORE THAN ONE VOICE?

Depending on the genre and/or delivery method—such as comedy, drama, education—you might find that you have more than one writing voice. You could be a teacher that writes workbooks while moonlighting as a novelist or joke book writer. You can "sound" both academic and casual, authoritative and friendly, formal or informal, young or mature. It all depends on your mood on the page and the type of material you're writing.

If you do notice a change in voice within the same writing project, make sure that each voice is appropriately placed. Beyond an exchange of character dialogue as well as those humorous moments in a dark drama that offer comic relief, a shift in tone and emotion can be confusing.

It's not common for two or more people to play the same person in a movie (although it has been done), but book content doesn't have that luxury unless there is more than one character or omnipresent being narrating the story. For each POV—point of view—there can be and should be a switch in voice. But if there's only one perspective, then the readers should find their rhythm within that voice quickly, easily enabling them to move at a comfortable pace.

Anything that abruptly halts the forward momentum of the reader is something you want to avoid. Bottom line: find your mainstay, your clearly present, most authentic voice, and let that be the strong foundation of your unique work.

One resource I found suggested three possible ways to create your own voice:

1. Just let it happen
2. Emulate someone else's voice
3. Design your voice from devices (*Writing Voice*, from the Editors of Writer's Digest, page 69)

I don't fully agree. While there's nothing wrong with emulating your favorite author's voice or writing with devices, neither of those will help you discover your very own exclusive voice. Dig into your own brain. Find what makes you different than your friends, family members, other writers in your sphere of influence, and established authors who have taken the time and energy to discover their own unusual tone.

If you try to sound like someone else, guess what happens? You sound like a copy, an impersonation—close cousin to a counterfeit. Yes, sometimes it's fun to hear someone trying to sound like someone else. It's amusing. A joke. But then we always return to the real thing to enjoy true originality. There's nothing like the real thing.

EXERCISE 6: *HEAR IT OUT LOUD*

This is a fun, enlightening exercise but one that writers rarely take the time to do.

Write a couple of pages of text and/or dialogue, then record it as you read it aloud (download an app on your phone for this if you don't already have one). Or better yet, have someone else read it aloud to you. See how it sounds. If you like what you hear, great. But if it seems awkward, unnatural, contrived, or forced, rewrite or edit it until it sounds genuine. Switch out "I am" for "I'm," "you are" for "you're," and "cannot" for "can't," and all the rest.

You'll start to hear the difference.

_____

_____

_____

_____

_____

_____

_____

_____

_____

_____

_____

_____

_____

_____

_____

_____

_____

_____

No Doubt–Readers Should Understand Your Meaning

Writing is an art, and within that medium we, as writers (and editors), have an obligation to speak a language people can comprehend. Fair enough? Now, what if our art begins to tilt until our words disfigure the picture we're painting on the page? For example: Van Gogh is one of the most brilliant artist minds ever, yet stare at one of his abstracts for long enough, and you'll begin to doubt reality. There's just enough there to kind of get what he was painting about, but the intricacies, the nuances, and subtlety of the topic fly right out the window.

Don't get me wrong, I'm not bashing good ol' Vincent. I'm just saying that taking poetic license shouldn't mean leaving your reader in your artistic dust.

Hemingway was a master at showing the reader aspects of the same things from different viewpoints. He used the simplest language with lots of repeated images and words, and every word counts. You can't remove even one without causing damage. You might characterize this voice as somewhat flat, restrained, weary, and absolutely under control. But that's his voice.

Poetry can be so lovely, so spiritual, so spontaneous, and so fantastically confusing. In a word, relevant—to the writer maybe, but not the reader. "Oh, soft pallet, swirling sentiment of delirious calm, silken streams floating on and on . . . and on . . . and on . . ." and *Oh, my gosh . . . where are we? Where were we going in the first place? I suddenly have no idea . . . make it stop!*

My point is it's better to be clear than to be conceptual. Don't lose your audience in the thick underbrush of your enchanted woods. At the very least, leave some breadcrumbs.

WRITING IS ART, PUBLISHING IS A BUSINESS

Now, some sobering specs: did you know that on Amazon there will be at least two million books published in the English language this year? That's on top of the two million from last year and the year before. And if you do a one-word search on a certain topic, tens of thousands or a hundred thousand results will appear. And just in the Christian market alone there are about four thousand books being published every month.

Last year, Amazon posted a new book every five minutes, and with everyone jumping on the bandwagon, that could change to every three minutes this year. I think you can see what I'm getting at. And with so many ways for people to publish their work now with multiple avenues in self-publishing while small traditional publishers and big mainstream publishers still crank out the titles, it can take a miracle for your book to be discovered.

Back before 1980, if you wrote something interesting and communicated it well, you got published and it sold. Even current bestselling authors sold more books fifteen or twenty years ago because there is now a plethora of different ways that people find their reading material. With bookstore shelves crammed to capacity, when a new book comes out (and bookstores decide to carry it), they'll give it about a two- to three-month window to see how it sells. If it does well, great. They'll move as many copies as the demand will allow.

However, if it doesn't sell, it goes back to the publisher, who puts it on a huge pallet, and it's sold to Amazon. Then Amazon will discount it to move the inventory. Personally, I think bookstores should be called browsing stores. A lot of people just go to visually sift through what's out there—eye candy—then go home and order online. That's how the brick and mortar stores came to a tragic end. I'm still grieving for all of the Mom & Pop stores that went under from about 2005 and beyond.

All of us on the industry side saw the old, faithful model breaking—and not all that slowly. Maybe we thought that it would somehow right itself, but things just kept sliding. Now, it's a whole new world of indie writers, bloggers, YouTube sensations, self-publishing tidal waves, and this is where we are.

After you pick yourself up off the floor, realize that with competition this fierce, the vast majority of those authors are poised at the same starting line you are waiting for the gun to go off. That's why you're taking the very first step in setting yourself apart from the rest. And that's good!

THINK TRIBE, NOT PLATFORM

Now, we've agreed that you need to stand out. You've already probably heard people talking about platforms. I don't particularly like the word *platform* because it indicates that you should be getting people to pay attention to only you. It's like you're up on a stage waving your arms madly saying, "Here I am! Look at me, look at me, right here . . . me on a platform!" But that goes against the personality traits of many writers I know. They're independent, quiet, sequestered (at times feeling a little isolated), and not used to the spotlight.

If you're not one to grandstand, I'd like to suggest that instead of building a platform, you should create a tribe of people—a community you can serve. Instead of your trying to get people to pay attention to you, you're actually out there spending time paying attention to others. Finding out what their needs are and how can you meet them.

Back to the notion that publishing is a business, your village paradigm is really just supply and demand. It's addressing the felt need of your audience, something that publisher committees discuss when reviewing potential books.

And you know the drill: Facebook, Twitter, Instagram, LinkedIn . . . social media presence that gets your name out there and people connecting with you—and you with them! Think of it as a group of like minds finding each other in 140-character smoke signals and touch-pad hieroglyphs. Your village can be whatever you want it to be, with those you care about and who care about you. Take the time to begin reaching out to people ready to join your special township. Your village is calling!

If you're ready to expand your reach, build a tribe, and gather a loyal audience, check out the Author Access MasterClass on my website: www.alicecrider.com.

THINK AND GO WRITE!

Oh, to be Hemmingway or Grisham or Seth Godin. But you're not, and guess what? I'm so glad. You are you, and that's awesome! Never tell an editor or an agent that you write like Donald Miller, Ann Voskamp, Francine Rivers, or Stephen King. You don't write like those authors because you can only write as *you* write. Your voice is completely your own and is only one part of your writing skill set. It's important, but it's not everything.

Aspire to write the best *you* can write. And the plan I have in mind for you is simple. First, you write. And then you write more. And then you keep writing. And one day, like a butterfly escaping a cocoon, a brand-new thought will take flight, and you'll be astonished at its intense color and contours.

That's your voice.

EXERCISE 7: PUSHING THE BOUNDARIES

If you look at the New York Times bestseller list (or any bestseller list), pretty much every book you find there is based on a unique thought, relevant concept, or idea.

For example, *Girl, Wash Your Face* by Rachel Hollis is based on the contemporary message of how women can break free from the world's predetermined expectations of them. Also, *The Great Alone* by Kristen Hannah tells of a 1970's Vietnam veteran, his wife, and young daughter who move off the grid to Alaska in an attempt to escape his demons only to discover that seclusion is more dangerous.

William Paul Young, author of *The Shack,* must have had a thought something like, "What if God looks like Whoopi Goldberg?" The author of *The Little Things,* Andy Andrews, talks about how he took a simple concept—don't sweat the small stuff—and turned it around completely, taking a totally opposite approach.

Try this: Write down an idea for a fictional story or nonfiction book.

_____

_____

_____

_____

_____

_____

_____

_____

_____

_____

_____

_____

_____

Now, boil it down to one sentence—one, that's all you get. And it shouldn't end up the size of a small paragraph.

_____

_____

_____

_____

You are consolidating, pushing down on the idea until only the meat remains. This exercise alone will hone skills that will come in very handy in order to focus on a single, strong concept.

After you've written down your sentence in a way that describes the story or idea effectively and completely as possible, it's time to elevate the concept. Switch the gender of the protagonist and see what happens. Turn the villain into the hero midway through the plot. Change your protagonist from human to animal. Animal to thing. Thing with a conscience . . . and so on.

Press against the walls of your comfort zone and see what emerges. Resist the borders of safe, sensible storytelling, and know that there are no margins you can't exceed. No electric fences or "Stay out!" signs to deter the explorer within you. For the love of the journey—push the boundaries. And keep pushing.

Listen . . . can you hear it? It's the sound of the irrepressible and unmistakable you!

CONCLUSION: WRITE ON!

I truly hope this book has addressed many of your questions concerning the value and necessity of discovering your voice on the page and more. Now, with the understanding of why voice is so important along with insight into target audience, the pitfalls of cliché, writing dynamic dialogue, economy of words, etc., you're really ahead of the game.

With so much at stake and millions of manuscripts making their way into the marketplace, why shouldn't yours rise to the top? There is only one reason I can think of outside of discovering your tribe and growing there. You've been too quiet by virtue of blending in with all the rest. But that was yesterday, and this is today. Silent no more!

We've covered a lot of ground, but with so much soul searching and the fundamental exercises to help shape and shade your voice, you're now ready to move confidently forward, taking your writing to the next level. Be brash! Be brave! Be true to who you are. There rests your strength—in the one-of-a-kind human that only your rare perspective and distinctive personality can offer. Your soul has something to say.

And when it does, you will finally and profoundly discover the wondrous voice of *you!*

APPENDIX A
ACTIVE VS. PASSIVE VERBS

Passive vs. Active Voice:
In active voice the subject of the sentence performs the action.

> Passive: The ball was thrown by Johnny.
> Active: Johnny threw the ball.

Weak vs. Strong Verbs:
Eliminate as many "to be" verbs as you can, and replace them with stronger verbs. [Hint: watch for *be, is, are, am, was, were, being*.]

NOTES

NOTES

NOTES

NOTES

NOTES